"I've been witness to the character of the people of America, who have shown calm in times of danger, compassion for one another, and toughness for the long haul. All of us have been partners in a great enterprise."

—President George W. Bush

Over the past eight years, President Bush has set
clear guiding principles, and applied those principles to
confront great challenges at home and abroad.

The following are highlights of the accomplishments from
the Administration of President George W. Bush
and Vice President Richard B. Cheney.

KEPT AMERICA SAFE AND PROMOTED LIBERTY ABROAD

Protecting the American people is the President's most solemn obligation. Since the terrorist attacks of 9/11, the President has carried with him a symbol of sacrifice and courage: a police shield given to him by the mother of an officer who died at the World Trade Center. As the President noted after the attack, "This is my reminder of lives that ended, and a task that does not end. . . . I will not yield; I will not rest; I will not relent in waging this struggle for freedom and security for the American people."

"The resolve of our great Nation is being tested. But make no mistake: We will show the world that we will pass this test."

President Bush, September 11, 2001

Waged the Global War on Terror

After 9/11, recognizing the ongoing threat posed by radical extremists, President Bush deployed all elements of national power to wage a global war on terror. The President enlisted a coalition of more than 90 nations to cooperate in a campaign to dismantle terrorist networks by drying up their financing, hunting down operatives, and bringing terrorist leaders to justice.

In this war on terror, America has taken the fight to the enemy. Hundreds of terrorists have been captured or killed in two dozen countries, including the mastermind of the 9/11 attacks—Khalid Sheikh Mohammed.

In **Afghanistan,** the United States and our allies removed the regime that harbored the terrorists who plotted the 9/11 attacks. As a result, more than 25 million Afghans are free; the terrorist training camps have been shut down; and Afghanistan has become an ally in the war on terror.

"War came to our shores on September the 11th, 2001. It was a war we did not ask for, it's a war we did not want, but it is a war that I intend to deal with so long as I'm your President."

President Bush, April 6, 2008

Today Afghanistan has a democratically elected President, a national assembly, and a market economy. Women are voting and starting their own businesses. Millions more children are in school, including girls who were once banned from the classroom. President Bush and President Karzai established the U.S.-Afghan Women's Council in 2002 to help give Afghan women the opportunity to improve their lives and rebuild their country. First Lady Laura Bush made three trips to Afghanistan to underscore America's commitment to this work. Although Afghanistan still faces serious challenges, the international community is working together to help this emerging democracy succeed.

In **Iraq,** the United States led a coalition to remove a dictator who murdered his own people, invaded his neighbors, and threatened the United States. Because our coalition acted to remove Saddam Hussein, 25 million Iraqis are free; the Iraqi people have the most progressive constitution in the Arab world; and Iraq has become an ally in the war on terror.

With Saddam Hussein gone from power, the coalition's mission turned to helping the Iraqi people defend their freedom against violent extremists. When the battle in Iraq reached a pivotal point, the President rejected calls for retreat. Instead, in January 2007, he ordered a new strategy supported by a **surge in forces.** This historic decision dramatically reduced violence and created the conditions for political and economic progress to take place.

One of the most dramatic outcomes was the transformation of **Anbar Province**, an area once reported by intelligence experts to be lost to al Qaeda. Local citizens took a stand against the terrorists, and an additional 4,000 Marines were sent to support them as part of the surge. As a result, the rule of law was restored in Anbar.

As conditions have improved across Iraq, America has reduced combat troops through the President's **Return on Success** plan. So far, all five surge brigade combat teams, two Marine battalions, and a Marine Expeditionary Unit have come home.

"Across the generations we have proclaimed the imperative of self-government, because no one is fit to be a master, and no one deserves to be a slave. Advancing these ideals is the mission that created our Nation. It is the honorable achievement of our fathers. Now it is the urgent requirement of our Nation's security, and the calling of our time."

President Bush, Second Inaugural Address

Did You Know?

- ✦ 9/11 mastermind Khalid Sheikh Mohammed was captured and is in custody.
- ✦ Iraqi forces have taken over security responsibilities from U.S. forces in more than two thirds of Iraqi provinces and helped reduce attacks to the lowest level in more than four years.
- ✦ More than six million children now attend Afghan schools, compared to fewer than one million in 2001; a third of these are girls who were previously barred from attending school.
- ✦ The Afghan economy has doubled since 2001.

Transformed the Institutions and Tools of War

President Bush has given our Nation the institutions and tools necessary for prevailing in the long struggle ahead. The President **retooled a Cold War-era Defense Department** into an agile, flexible, and adaptive organization. The President increased defense funding 73 percent to dramatically expand America's all-volunteer force and purchase advanced technologies, such as unmanned aerial vehicles. The National Guard was elevated from a strategic reserve to an operational reserve. The Defense Department modified the military command structure by creating U.S. Northern Command and U.S. Africa Command. Additionally, other reforms have bolstered efforts to combat the danger of weapons of mass destruction and have allowed special operations forces to better confront emerging challenges.

"We will direct every resource at our command to win the war against terrorists: every means of diplomacy, every tool of intelligence, every instrument of law enforcement, every financial influence. We will starve the terrorists of funding, turn them against each other, rout them out of their safe hiding places, and bring them to justice."

President Bush, September 24, 2001

President Bush improved our country's intelligence-gathering capabilities. The President worked with Congress to enact four major pieces of legislation: 1. **The USA Patriot Act**; 2. **The Intelligence Reform and Terrorism Prevention Act**; 3. **The Protect America Act**; and 4. **Modernization of the Foreign Intelligence Surveillance Act**. The President established the **Director of National Intelligence**, tore down the "wall" that once divided law enforcement and intelligence operations, created the **National Counterterrorism Center**, and shifted the focus of the **FBI** from investigating terrorist attacks to preventing them.

The President also bolstered America's homeland security. More than 20 Federal agencies were merged together to create **the Department of Homeland Security (DHS)**. This department provided more than $27 billion in homeland security grants to cities and States to strengthen response capabilities and information-sharing and to protect critical infrastructure, such as chemical and nuclear facilities. The Administration also worked with cities and States to create **interagency response plans** to ensure clear lines of responsibility in the event of another attack.

To protect the homeland, President Bush also increased funding for border security and immigration enforcement efforts by more than 160 percent. As a result, the number of **Border Patrol** agents has doubled to more than 18,000 agents. The Border Patrol has been equipped with better technology. The practice of "catch and release" was effectively ended at our borders, and a program was created to screen foreign travelers using biometrics and other 21st Century technology.

After 9/11, the Administration also strengthened airport security. The **Transportation Security Administration** was created to screen every commercial air passenger in the country, and the number of Federal marshals on passenger flights increased.

The Administration improved **security at our ports**. Nearly 100 percent of cargo containers that arrive at America's ports are now screened for radiological and nuclear threats, and the people who load and unload these containers are credentialed through a special program. Through an international program, the vast majority of shipments entering our ports are screened at foreign ports long before they dock in our waters.

To combat the threat of biological and chemical attacks, the Administration created a new **air monitoring system** that is now operating in 30 American cities. This new system is designed to detect harmful biological agents and accelerate the government's response. The Administration also increased America's **stockpile of vaccines and antibiotics** to prepare our Nation for a biological attack or other health emergency.

"In this new century, there is a great divide between those who place no value on human life, and rejoice in the suffering of others, and those who believe that every life has matchless value, and answer suffering with compassion and kindness. The contrast is vivid—and the position of America is clear. We will lead the cause of freedom, justice, and hope, because both our values and our interests demand it…We also know that nations with free, healthy, prosperous people will be sources of stability, not breeding grounds for extremists and hate and terror."

President Bush, December 14, 2006

The President led an international campaign against terrorist financing and money laundering and created the **Office of Terrorism and Financial Intelligence at the Treasury Department** to lead efforts that have made it harder, costlier, and riskier for al Qaeda and like-minded allies to raise and move money around the world.

Together, all these measures have helped close critical intelligence gaps and provided America's law enforcement and intelligence communities with much-needed tools for preventing acts of terror. More than seven years have passed without another attack on our soil. This is not for lack of trying on the part of the terrorists. Since 9/11, the United States and our allies have stopped deadly terrorist plots, including a 2002 plot to hijack an airplane and fly it into the tallest skyscraper in Los Angeles, a 2003 plot to hijack and crash planes into targets on the East Coast, and a 2006 plot to blow up multiple passenger jets traveling from London.

Did You Know?

- President Bush implemented the largest reorganization of the Federal national security apparatus since 1947.
- More than 400 individuals and entities that posed a threat to America had assets frozen, transactions blocked, or were isolated from the U.S. financial system.
- The increase in defense funding is the largest increase since the Truman Administration.
- Intelligence experts believe the 2006 plot to blow up multiple passenger jets traveling from London was only weeks from being carried out.

Advanced Missile Defense and Counterproliferation

President Bush took unprecedented measures to prevent weapons of mass destruction (WMD) from falling into hands of our enemies. The President launched a global threat reduction program that has removed enough material for more than 30 nuclear bombs from sites around the world. Under the Global Initiative to Combat Nuclear Terrorism, a coalition of **75 nations** is working together to enhance protection, detection, and response to nuclear terrorism. This Administration also worked with our allies to shut down dangerous proliferation networks.

President Bush persuaded Libya to disclose and dismantle all aspects of its WMD and advanced missile programs and renounce terrorism. The Administration dismantled the A.Q. Khan nuclear proliferation network, which had previously spread sensitive nuclear technology and capability to Iran and North Korea. Through the Six-Party talks, the United States worked to secure a commitment from North Korea to abandon its nuclear weapons and its nuclear weapons program. And by working with our partners in the international community, America increased pressure on Iran to abandon its pursuit of uranium enrichment activities.

To protect against the danger of rogue regimes armed with ballistic missiles, the Administration withdrew from the **Anti-Ballistic Missile Treaty** and made missile defense operational. The Administration also concluded agreements with the Czech Republic and Poland to host missile defense sites that will help protect America and our allies.

Did You Know?

+ This Administration halved the U.S. nuclear weapons stockpile by 2007— five years ahead of schedule.
+ The President's Proliferation Security Initiative united more than 90 nations to cooperate to stop of the spread of weapons of mass destruction, their delivery systems, and related materials.
+ The United States persuaded the UN Security Council to require all UN members to take enforcement actions against the proliferation of WMD and related materials.

Established the Freedom Agenda to Spread Hope Through Liberty

In the long run, expanding liberty and democracy is the best way to defeat extremists and their ideology of hatred. So under President Bush's leadership, the United States has worked to aid the rise of free societies around the world. In countries from **Lebanon**, to **Ukraine**, to **Georgia**, America supported successful democratic revolutions. In **Pakistan**, America supported elections that reflected the will of the people. In the Balkans, America recognized **Kosovo** as an independent country. In the Holy Land, President Bush became the first American President to support a two-state solution with a **democratic Israel and a democratic Palestine** living side-by-side in peace. And around the globe, President Bush more than doubled funding for the promotion of democracy.

Brave **democratic reformers and dissidents** from Damascus to Tehran to Havana have found a true ally in President Bush. The President has met with activists from more than 35 countries. He has spoken out against human rights abuses, called for the release of political prisoners by repressive regimes, and candidly pressed nations with whom America has good relations for greater freedoms, such as Egypt, Saudi Arabia, and China. President Bush has also applied tough sanctions on the regimes of Belarus, Cuba, Zimbabwe, and Burma, where Mrs. Bush has also been a leading advocate for human rights. This Administration also led the international response to the genocide in **Darfur**.

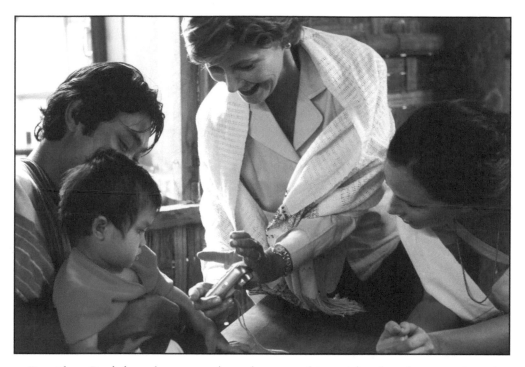

President Bush has also strengthened partnerships with other democracies. An expanded **NATO Alliance** is now deploying on important missions across the world in defense of freedom. The United States completed a historic **civil nuclear agreement** with India, reshaping the relationship between the world's two largest democracies. And thanks to new agreements and alliances with the European Union, Central America, Japan, South Korea, Australia, Singapore, and Brazil, the world is more secure.

Did You Know?

+ The President increased the budget for the National Endowment for Democracy by more than 150 percent since 2001.
+ The United States provided more than $1.5 billion in new funding for humanitarian and peacekeeping aid to Darfur.
+ President Bush directed all senior U.S. officials serving in undemocratic countries to maintain regular contact with political dissidents and democracy activists to help give them a voice.

Established a New Approach to International Development

The Administration ushered in a new era in development assistance by doubling funding and transforming the way it is delivered. Through new development assistance tools such as the Millennium Challenge Account, governments that accept U.S. assistance are held accountable for making democratic and economic reforms to increase transparency, strengthen their economies, improve the lives of their citizens, and ultimately decrease their dependence on aid.

> *"For decades, the success of development aid was measured only in the resources spent, not the results achieved. . . . We must accept a higher, more difficult, more promising call. Developed nations have a duty not only to share our wealth, but also to encourage sources that produce wealth: economic freedom, political liberty, the rule of law, and human rights."*
>
> President Bush, March 22, 2002

The **President's Emergency Plan for AIDS Relief** (PEPFAR) is the largest commitment by any nation to combat a single disease in history. Since the President launched this initiative in 2003, PEPFAR has supported life-saving treatment for more than 2.1 million people and care for more than 10.1 million people worldwide. The Program was reauthorized in 2008, and under this legislation the next phase of the program will support treatment for a total of at least three million people, the prevention of 12 million new infections, and care for 12 million people, including five million orphans and vulnerable children.

The **President's Malaria Initiative** (PMI) is on track to reduce malaria deaths by half in 15 targeted countries across Sub-Saharan Africa. In 2007 alone, the PMI reached more than 25 million people with lifesaving treatment and prevention services, and this good work continues. America's also became the first and largest contributor to the **Global Fund To Fight AIDS, Tuberculosis, and Malaria**. America also expanded an initiative to treat more than 300 million people in Africa, Asia, and Latin America suffering from seven major neglected tropical diseases.

The results-based **Millennium Challenge Corporation** (MCC) is investing in countries that fight corruption, govern justly, and invest in the health and education of their people. Millennium Challenge programs have invested $6.7 billion in 35 countries around the world. Among other benefits, these investments strengthen relationships and create new markets for U.S. exports.

The President extended the **African Growth and Opportunity Act** (AGOA). AGOA assists African countries in building their exports while creating markets for U.S. exports. The **African Financial Sector Initiative** encouraged the financial community to create several new private equity funds, which helped mobilize nearly $2 billion in private investment for Africa.

The Bush Administration dramatically increased funding to send children in the developing world to school through programs such as the **African Education Initiative**. This initiative increased education opportunities for more than 34 million children.

"We fight against poverty because faith requires it and conscience demands it. And we fight against poverty with a growing conviction that major progress is within our reach."

President Bush, March 22, 2002

During this Administration, America led the world in providing **food aid and natural disaster relief**. In addition to feeding the hungry, the United States helped lead relief efforts after the Southeast Asian tsunami, the cyclone in Burma, and the tropical storms that devastated Caribbean and Central American countries.

Did You Know?

+ Since 2001, the United States has provided $16 billion in food aid.
+ The MCC has now signed agreements, which seek transformational change in the development of recipient countries, for $6.7 billion in grant funding for 35 countries.
+ The President committed $1 billion through the African Education Initiative and the Initiative for Expanded Education for the World's Poorest Children to educate children in poor nations.
+ The United States has provided $10 billion for international disaster relief and other humanitarian efforts since 2001.

LOWERED TAXES & INSTITUTED PRO-GROWTH POLICIES

President Bush enacted the **largest tax relief in a generation**. For only the third time in history, Americans received across-the-board tax relief. Tax rates fell for everyone who pays income taxes, and more than 13 million Americans saw their income taxes eliminated altogether. The President worked with Congress to double the child tax credit, reduce the marriage penalty, and put the death tax on the road to extinction.

"It's your money. Tax relief will give you a chance to set your priorities for your family. It says that we in the Federal government have a fundamental trust in the people of America, and that's where our faith should be—in the people."

President Bush, February 20, 2001

President Bush also worked with Congress to reduce tax rates on dividends and long-term capital gains. Since these policies went into effect, capital gains have increased nearly 150 percent, and dividend income growth has increased from an average annual rate of about 8.5 percent to more than 14 percent. These pro-growth policies helped America's economy emerge from the recession that President Bush inherited when he entered office in 2001. America's economy rebounded with six years of uninterrupted economic growth and an unprecedented 52 consecutive months of job creation.

At the end of his Administration, the President responded to new economic challenges. When the housing market began to decline in 2007, the President moved aggressively to help struggling families keep their homes. The Administration launched FHA Secure and implemented Hope for Homeowners to help families move into government-backed mortgages. The Administration helped facilitate the formation of the HOPE NOW Alliance to coordinate private sector efforts to help homeowners. Together, these efforts have helped more than two million American families so far.

When the overall economy began to slow in early 2008, the President worked with Congress to enact a **$150 billion growth package**. This package delivered rebates to individuals and families and provided incentives for businesses to make new investments.

"We must trust American workers to compete with anyone in the world and empower them by opening up new markets overseas. Today, our economic growth increasingly depends on our ability to sell American goods and crops and services all over the world. So we're working to break down barriers to trade and investment wherever we can."

President Bush, January 28, 2008

When our Nation faced an unprecedented financial crisis in September, the President called for an unprecedented response. He rallied Members of Congress to enact a $700 billion rescue plan to avert a global financial meltdown. And together with leaders from around the world, whom he convened in Washington, D.C., in November, the President has worked to restore stability to our financial system and return our economy to the path of prosperity and growth.

In the long run, the future of our economy depends in large part on opening new markets for American goods, services, and crops. When President Bush took office in 2001, the United States had free trade agreements (FTAs) in force with only three countries. Today, America has agreements in force with 14 countries, and Congress has approved FTAs with another three. These agreements have benefited American farmers, workers, and small business owners. For example, after the **Dominican Republic-Central America-United States Free Trade Agreement** (CAFTA-DR) came into force, U.S. exports to Central America increased dramatically. Thanks in part to President Bush's leadership on free trade, America's exports now account for a larger percentage of our Gross Domestic Product than at any other time on record.

In the 21st century global economy, America's spirit of innovation is one of our country's greatest advantages. To unleash this spirit, President Bush launched the **American Competitiveness Initiative**. The Federal government has increased its investment in research and development to a record $143 billion – an increase of 57 percent from 2001.

Throughout their Administration, President Bush and Vice President Cheney emphasized the importance of spending taxpayer dollars wisely. While always ensuring that the men and women responsible for protecting America received all the resources they needed, the President presided over a dramatic reduction in the rate of growth of non-security **discretionary spending** from 16 percent in 2001 to less than three percent today.

President Bush also instituted policies that reduced wasteful Federal spending, saved taxpayers billions of dollars, and brought greater accountability and effectiveness to the Federal Government.

Over the past five years, nearly $40 billion in taxpayer money has been saved by ending or reforming ineffective federal programs. And by increasing accountability, federal agencies have reduced **improper payments by $8 billion** since 2004.

To protect taxpayer dollars, this Administration shined a bright light on the Congressional practice of slipping pet projects, known as **earmarks**, into legislation at the last minute out of public view. President Bush established the website earmarks. omb.gov to bring thousands of earmark projects totaling tens of billions of dollars into public view.

To protect taxpayer dollars, the President also launched the USASpending.gov website. This site provides visitors with information about Federal contracts, grants, loans, and other types of government spending.

Did You Know?

+ The President's tax relief helped fuel growth that led to the largest three-year increase in revenues in 26 years.
+ A family of four earning $40,000 kept an average of $2,000 more of their own money in 2007 thanks to the President's tax relief.
+ Americans with the highest incomes—the top five percent—pay a greater share of the total Federal income tax burden today than they did before the President's tax relief.
+ Growth in exports, to a record $1.6 trillion, accounted for about half of U.S. economic growth in 2007.
+ U.S. agriculture exports were $92.4 billion in 2007, up 74 percent from 2000.
+ After-tax per-capita income increased 12 percent from 2000 to 2007.

REFORMED GOVERNMENT TO BETTER SERVE AMERICANS

Brought Greater Accountability to Schools and Delivered Results for Students

President Bush's focus on accountability transformed America's education system by replacing a culture of low expectations for some with a commitment to high achievement for all. The President worked with Members of Congress from both sides of the aisle to pass the landmark **No Child Left Behind** (NCLB) Act. This law asks states to set measurable standards and hold schools accountable for ensuring every child learns to read and do math at grade level. Six years after NCLB became law, the results are clear. According to the Nation's Report Card, fourth-grade students achieved their highest reading and math scores on record, and eighth-grade students achieved their highest math scores on record. African-American and Hispanic students posted all-time highs in reading and math, and the achievement gap has narrowed.

"It's easy to set low expectations. . . . That's the easy way out. What No Child Left Behind says is that we're going to take the hard way. We're going to set high standards, and then we're going to measure to determine whether or not those standards are being met."

President Bush, January 7, 2008

NCLB has also provided parents with valuable information about how schools are performing. When schools fall short of standards, the law empowers parents with options, such as transferring their children to a better public school or enrolling them in free tutoring. To further expand options for parents, the Administration has provided funding to more than half of all public charter schools. And working with Congress, the Administration created the first Federal private school-choice program. Through **D.C. Opportunity Scholarships**, families in our Nation's capital can now choose to send their children to a private school, including a religious school.

Did You Know?

+ NCLB helped increase the percentage of first graders reading at grade level in 44 of 50 States.
+ President Bush created a $100 million Teacher Incentive Fund to reward teachers who improve student achievement in high-need school districts.
+ 1.2 million more students are attending college in the 2008-09 year compared to 2001-02 thanks to a near doubling of Pell Grant funding to $16.2 billion and an increase of the largest maximum Pell Grant award to $4,700.
+ The number of charter schools in the United States has doubled since 2000, thanks in part to an infusion of Federal funding.

Instituted Market-Oriented Health Care Programs & Prescription Drug Benefit

The President worked with Congress to create the groundbreaking **Medicare Prescription Drug Benefit**. Under this program, private drug plans compete against each other to provide coverage for beneficiaries. This competition has helped drive down prices. The average premiums in 2008 were 40 percent lower than the original estimates. Overall, the projected spending for the program between 2004 and 2013 is 38 percent lower than originally expected—a reduction of about $240 billion.

The Administration also expanded consumer choice and competition for health care in other areas. Through the **Medicare Advantage** program, more Medicare recipients have chosen the option of a private plan for their health care coverage. Through **Health Saving Accounts** (HSAs), Americans of all ages have put away money for routine medical expenses free of taxes. The number of individuals covered by HSA-eligible plans at small businesses increased by 70 percent in 2008. The President also increased transparency of health care pricing and quality of care and launched an initiative to make electronic health records available to most Americans within 10 years.

Did You Know?

+ Nearly 10 million Americans are enrolled in private Medicare Advantage programs, and virtually every county in America has a private plan option.
+ Among seniors, the satisfaction rate with the drug benefit is close to 90 percent.
+ The President added preventive screening to Medicare to help diagnose illnesses earlier.
+ Since 2001, more than 1,200 community health centers have opened or expanded nationwide.
+ Nearly seven million more Americans now have coverage in HSA-eligible plans.

Improved Lives by Partnering With Faith-Based and Community Groups

America's faith-based and community organizations play an important role in confronting problems like poverty, hunger, and disease. Unfortunately, for many years, these organizations struggled to compete for federal funds. So the President created the **Faith-Based and Community Initiative** (FBCI) to level the playing field and empower America's armies of compassion.

"The Administration has upheld its promise to treat community and faith-based organizations as trusted partners. We've held your organizations to high standard and insisted on clear results. And your organizations have delivered on those results. You've helped revolutionize the way government addresses the greatest challenges facing our society."

President Bush, June 27, 2008

This initiative has produced incredible results. It has supported the recovery of more than 200,000 substance abuse addicts, matched more than 100,000 children of prisoners with mentors, and provided former inmates with the tools to make a new and more hopeful start on life. Partnerships with faith-based and community groups have helped homeless Americans find a safe place to stay. These efforts have contributed to more than 50,000 individuals moving from shelters and streets to a new residence. And through partnerships with local non-profits, which have been central to providing care for more than 10 million people affected by HIV/AIDS, the President's Emergency Plan for AIDS Relief reflects the vision of the FBCI by supporting efforts of grassroots organizations to tackle community health needs.

Throughout his Administration, the President has challenged Americans to build communities of service and a Nation of character. Following the attacks of September 11th, 2001, the President called on all Americans to spend at least 4,000 hours in service to our country over their lifetime. The President also created USA Freedom Corps to help connect Americans with opportunities for service. The American people have responded by volunteering in record numbers.

Did You Know?

+ The President's first Executive Order established the White House Office of Faith-Based and Community Initiatives. Similar offices were established at 11 Federal agencies, and 35 Governors now have State offices or liaisons of their own.
+ More than 515,000 children received after-school tutoring through Supplemental Educational Services, many from faith-based and community providers.
+ In response to Hurricane Katrina, National Service programs have given more than 5.4 million hours of service, directing 405,000 volunteers in recovery efforts.
+ In 2007 alone, more than 2,200, or 87 percent, of partners in the President's Emergency Plan for AIDS Relief were indigenous groups, and nearly one-quarter were faith-based.

Provided Unprecedented Resources for Those Who Defended Our Freedom

President Bush honored our solemn commitment to care for those who have served in uniform. During his Administration, the President nearly doubled funding for the **Department of Veterans Affairs.** The President expanded grants to help homeless veterans in all 50 states, because veterans who served in distant lands should not have to live without shelter in the land they fought to defend. The number of homeless veterans dropped nearly 40 percent between 2001 and 2007. The President also signed a GI Bill for the 21st century. This legislation significantly expanded education benefits and allowed those who have defended our country to transfer unused benefits to their spouses or children. The President also signed legislation and issued regulations amending the Family Medical Leave Act to permit family members of injured service members to take additional time away from their jobs to care for their loved one.

"Caring for our veterans is a solemn responsibility of the Federal government. It is our enduring pledge to every man and woman who puts on our Nation's uniform."

President Bush, October 30, 2007

President Bush also worked to help America's wounded warriors build lives of hope, promise, and dignity. Over the past three years, the VA has dedicated more than a billion dollars to support traumatic brain injury and post-traumatic stress disorder research and treatment. President Bush repealed a century-old provision to ensure that military retirees with severe disabilities receive both their military retirement pay and VA disability compensation. The President also oversaw other important reforms including implementing recommendations from the Dole-Shalala commission he established.

Did You Know?

+ The President committed more than $6 billion to modernize and expand VA facilities.
+ VA's polytrauma system of care was expanded to 22 network sites and clinic support teams to provide state-of-the-art treatment to injured veterans closer to home.
+ Under this Administration, DoD, in cooperation with VA, created the Defense Centers of Excellence for Psychological Health and Traumatic Brain Injury to take advantage of cutting-edge medical technology.

SET A BRIGHT COURSE FOR AMERICA'S FUTURE

Advanced Energy Production

President Bush worked to reduce America's dependence on oil. In 2005, the President signed an energy bill that established a national Renewable Fuels standard to encourage greater use of fuels like ethanol and biodiesel. In 2007, the President called for modernizing fuel economy standards and increasing alternative fuels. Later that year, the President signed the Energy Independence and Security Act into law. This legislation established a national fuel economy standard of 35 miles per gallon by 2020 and will help save billions of gallons of fuel. This legislation also mandated a five-fold increase in the use of renewable fuels by 2022.

"America is the kind of country that when [we] see a problem, we address it head-on. I've set a great goal for our country, and that is to reduce our dependence on oil by investing in technologies that will produce abundant supplies of clean and renewable energy, and at the same time show the world that we're good stewards of the environment."

President Bush, March 5, 2008

The President also encouraged the development of a new generation of clean energy technologies. The Administration committed nearly $18 billion to promote new ways of powering our automobiles and generating electricity, such as biofuels, hydrogen fuel cells, nuclear power, and wind and solar energy. The President also signed legislation giving the Department of Energy the authority to provide up to $67.5 billion in loans and loan guarantees to help support innovative energy projects for reducing greenhouse gas or air pollutant emissions and for retooling auto plants to produce more efficient vehicles.

When gas prices soared in 2008, President Bush lifted the executive prohibition on offshore exploration for oil and gas. This will create a tremendous opportunity to expand domestic production. At the urging of this Administration and with widespread support from the public, Congress also removed its ban on offshore exploration.

Did You Know?

+ Ethanol production quadrupled from 2000 to 2007, and nearly $1 billion was invested to advance cellulosic ethanol made from switchgrass, wood chips, and other non-food sources.
+ This Administration launched the Nuclear Power 2010 Program and other significant efforts that helped encourage industry to submit 17 applications for 26 new nuclear reactors in the United States.
+ The President's $2 billion commitment to the Coal Research Initiative was fulfilled three years early.
+ $1.2 billion was invested in hydrogen and fuel cell vehicle research and development.

Protected the Environment

Throughout his Administration, President Bush made protecting the environment for future generations a top priority.

President Bush worked to improve air quality. Between 2001 and 2007, air pollution fell 12 percent. This Administration put in place new air quality standards that are the most stringent in history as well as new rules that will cut diesel engine emissions by 90 percent. Policies like these will help produce even more dramatic cuts in air pollution in the years ahead.

The President worked to protect our forests. In 2002, he launched the Healthy Forest Initiative. This initiative improved and protected more than 27 million acres of Federal forests and grasslands and helped protect communities from catastrophic fires.

President Bush worked to preserve our wetlands. In 2004, the President announced the Wetlands Initiative to protect, restore, or improve three million acres of wetlands by 2009. When that goal was met a year early in 2008, a new goal was launched to protect four million additional acres over the next five years.

The President worked with America's farmers and ranchers to protect our Nation's soil, wildlife, and water. Under the Conservation Reserve Program, the Administration re-enrolled and extended contracts covering 28 million acres.

President Bush worked to protect ocean and coastal ecosystems. Through the Oceanic Action Plan, the Administration worked to end overfishing, advance marine science, and educate the public about the need for preservation. The President also designated nearly 140,000 square miles of the Northwestern Hawaiian Islands as a Marine National Monument. Today, this monument is the world's largest fully protected marine area.

President Bush worked to confront climate change through a rational and balanced approach. The President put our Nation on track to reduce greenhouse gas intensity 18 percent by 2012 and set a goal to stop the growth of greenhouse gas emissions by 2025. To help reach this goal, the Administration has advanced a series of new Federal mandates, tens of billions of dollars in incentives, and innovative technology partnerships.

Did You Know?

+ Between 2001 and 2008, the United States committed more than $22 billion total to climate change technology research.
+ The new Papahānaumokuākea Marine National Monument protects more than 7,000 species.
+ More than 220 Preserve America grants were awarded in more than 650 communities in all 50 States to protect America's cultural and natural heritage.
+ Record funding was provided to repair and improve our national parks through the President's National Parks Centennial Initiative, a priority of First Lady Laura Bush.

Reduced Crime, Lowered Teen Drug Use, and Protected Vulnerable Children

During this Administration, the overall incidence of reported crime reached its lowest level in decades. Thanks in part to the creation of Project Safe Neighborhoods and innovative programs for enforcing Federal firearm laws, the overall rate of reported crimes reached a 30-year low in 2007. The government also moved aggressively to prosecute those who committed corporate fraud and corruption. Overall, Federal prosecutors secured nearly 1,300 convictions for corporate fraud.

Under President Bush's leadership, the Administration developed an effective National Drug Control Strategy for reducing teenage drug use. Since 2001, the number of American teenagers using drugs has declined by nearly 900,000—a 25 percent reduction. In addition, the Administration has helped dismantle more than 5,000 drug trafficking organizations.

> *"Our nation has made this commitment: Anyone who targets a child for harm will be a primary target of law enforcement."*
>
> President Bush, October 23, 2002

Under President Bush's leadership, the Administration took steps to protect children from sexual predators. In 2003, the Administration launched the Innocence Lost Initiative to combat childhood prostitution. Since the start of this initiative, more than 575 children have been rescued from sexual exploitation and more than 300 defendants have been convicted. To combat predators on the Internet, the Administration created Project Safe Childhood and expanded the Internet Crimes Against Children program. The expansion of this program helped lead to the apprehension of more than 2,350 suspected child predators in Fiscal Year 2007—a 15 percent increase from Fiscal Year 2006.

Did You Know?

+ A national network of 59 Federally funded regional task forces was created to investigate computer-related child sexual exploitation.
+ President Bush signed the PROTECT Act, which gave law enforcement new tools to prevent, investigate, and prosecute violent crimes against children and increased the punishment for these crimes.
+ Federal prosecutions of child predators jumped nearly 30 percent in 2007.
+ This Administration awarded approximately $10 billion to support local housing and service programs that contributed to the decline in homelessness.

STOOD ON PRINCIPLE & SHOWED THE WAY AHEAD

Promoted a Culture of Life

The President worked to build a culture where every human being is welcomed in life and protected in law. The President signed legislation banning the abhorrent procedure known as partial birth abortion, and his Administration successfully defended the law before the Supreme Court. The President also signed legislation extending legal protection to children who are born despite abortion attempts and allowing prosecutors to charge those who harm or kill a pregnant woman with harming or killing her unborn child as well. The Administration took steps to protect the rights of health care providers to act according to their conscience. Additionally, by restoring the Mexico City Policy, President Bush also ensured that America's international family planning organizations do not indirectly subsidize abortion.

The President helped empower doctors and scientists to pursue new medical treatments while respecting ethical boundaries. This Administration became the first in history to make federal funds available for embryonic stem cell research, but this historic step was taken in a way that did not encourage the destruction of human embryos. Subsequent research has shown that adult skin-cells have the potential to be reprogrammed to act like embryonic stems cells. This discovery supports the President's principle that our Nation can advance the boundaries of science while maintaining a culture of life.

Appointed Judges Committed to Ruling by the Letter of the Law

President Bush kept his promise to appoint judges who strictly interpret the law instead of legislating from the bench. The President appointed John Roberts and Samuel Alito to the Supreme Court of the United States. Overall, the President's appointees now account for more than one third of all active Federal judges.

Showed Leadership on Reforms of Entitlement Programs and Immigration

The greatest long-term challenge to America's fiscal health is the unsustainable growth of entitlement programs like Medicare, Medicaid, and Social Security. The President recognized these challenges and proposed innovative solutions to confront them. While the Congress failed to act on these proposals, President Bush succeeded in raising awareness about this important issue.

On immigration, President Bush proposed a comprehensive plan for reform. This plan recognized that America is both a nation of laws and a nation of immigrants. It included provisions for securing America's borders, creating a temporary worker program, holding employers accountable, and addressing the status of illegal immigrants already living in the United States. While the Congress did not pass the President's proposals, they will help shape the debate over immigration reform for years to come. Even without this legislation, actions taken during this Administration have increased employer accountability for hiring practices, put in place hundreds of miles of tactical infrastructure, and increased staffing at the border. These actions have slowed the flow of illegal immigrants into this country and have set the stage for the next Administration to tackle this difficult issue.

President Bush led with a hopeful vision, met complex and rapid-fire challenges with steady resolve, and based his decisions on principle.

Asked how he thinks he'll be remembered, he said:

"I think I'll be remembered as a guy who was dealt some pretty tough issues and I dealt with them head-on and I didn't try to shy away. I helped this country protect itself, and at the same time was unabashed at spreading certain values to others— the main one being liberty."

100 Things
Americans May Not Know
About the Bush Administration Record

100 THINGS AMERICANS MAY NOT KNOW ABOUT THE BUSH ADMINISTRATION RECORD

KEPT AMERICA SAFE

+ For more than seven years after September 11, 2001, prevented another attack on our homeland.

Waged the Global War on Terror

+ Removed threatening regimes in Iraq and Afghanistan, which freed 50 million people.
+ Weakened the al-Qaeda network and its affiliates.
+ Disrupted terrorist plots and built a coalition of more than 90 nations to fight terrorism.

Transformed Our Approach to Combating Terrorism After the 9/11 Attacks

+ Transformed the United States military and retooled the Department of Defense to meet 21st century challenges.
+ Established the Director of National Intelligence, the National Counterterrorism Center, the Department of Homeland Security, and the Homeland Security Council. Shifted the FBI's focus from investigating terrorist attacks to preventing them.
+ Advocated for and signed the Patriot Act, the Intelligence Reform and Terrorism Prevention Act, and a modernization of the Foreign Intelligence Surveillance Act.

Protected the United States Homeland

+ Arrested and convicted terrorists in the United States and captured and isolated key financiers and facilitators of terrorism.
+ Expanded the Border Patrol and improved border security.
+ Created the Transportation Security Administration, built a consolidated watchlist program, and strengthened programs for screening individuals entering the United States.
+ Provided approximately $27 billion in homeland security grants, increased national preparedness, protected key infrastructure, and strengthened the capabilities of all levels of government.

+ Improved cargo screening and security at U.S. ports and increased containerized cargo screening overseas.
+ Invested more than $38 billion in public health and medical systems, created a biothreat air monitoring system, and developed a national strategy and international partnership on avian and pandemic flu.

Advanced Missile Defense and Counterproliferation Efforts, and Prevented our Enemies from Threatening America and our Allies with Weapons of Mass Destruction (WMD)

+ Secured a commitment from North Korea to end its nuclear weapons program.
+ Persuaded Libya to disclose and dismantle all aspects of its WMD and advanced missile programs and renounce terrorism.
+ Withdrew from the Anti-Ballistic Missile Treaty and operationalized missile defense.
+ Dismantled the A.Q. Khan nuclear proliferation network.
+ Established the Proliferation Security Initiative and multilateral coalitions to stop WMD proliferation and strengthen our ability to locate and secure nuclear and radiological materials around the world.
+ Halved the U.S. nuclear weapons stockpile five years ahead of schedule.

PROMOTED LIBERTY ABROAD

Removed Totalitarian Regimes in Afghanistan and Iraq and Helped Transform Both Nations into Emerging Democracies and Allies in the War on Terror

+ Helped establish an emerging democratic Afghan government and helped improve the lives of the Afghan people, especially women and children.
+ Helped establish an emerging democratic Iraqi government and the Iraqi Army, and ordered the surge of U.S. forces, which dramatically reduced violence and created the conditions for political and economic progress.
+ Established innovative programs, such as Provincial Reconstruction Teams, to help create the conditions for peace and security in Iraq and Afghanistan.

Created Institutions to Propel the Spread of Democracy Worldwide, Helped Oppressed People Secure their Freedom, and Strengthened Support for Dissidents and Democracy Activists

+ Created international organizations to promote the spread of freedom abroad and more than doubled funding to promote democracy worldwide.

+ Generated international pressure to end the Syrian occupation of Lebanon and helped restore democracy and civilian rule in Pakistan.
+ Supported the development of democracy in Ukraine and Georgia and helped establish Kosovo as an independent, multi-ethnic democracy.
+ Focused international attention and applied tough sanctions on oppressive regimes in Burma, Belarus, Zimbabwe, and other nations, and bolstered civil society activists in countries such as Cuba and Venezuela.

Confronted Threats and Helped Defuse Regional Conflicts

+ Worked with our international partners to confront Iran's destructive policies and to pressure Iran to suspend nuclear enrichment.
+ Laid the foundation for a future Israeli-Palestinian peace agreement and a democratic Palestinian state by launching direct negotiations between Israel and the Palestinian Authority (PA) at the Annapolis Conference and working with the PA to build accountable institutions.
+ Led the international response to the genocide in Darfur and worked to end major conflicts in Africa.

HELPED MILLIONS OF PEOPLE AROUND THE WORLD THROUGH A NEW APPROACH TO DEVELOPMENT

+ Doubled foreign assistance worldwide and transformed our foreign assistance programs to increase transparency and hold governments accountable for making democratic and economic reforms.
+ Helped save millions of lives through the President's Emergency Plan for AIDS Relief and the President's Malaria Initiative.
+ Committed $350 million over five years to treat more than 300 million people suffering from seven neglected tropical diseases and became the first, and largest, contributor to the Global Fund to Fight AIDS, Tuberculosis, and Malaria.
+ Created the Millennium Challenge Corporation, which holds recipient countries of foreign aid accountable to make political and economic reforms, expanded the African Growth and Opportunity Act, and provided debt relief to impoverished nations.
+ Created programs that will help educate more than 65 million children in the developing world.
+ Provided more than $16 billion for global food aid and more than $10 billion for disaster relief and other humanitarian efforts worldwide since 2001.

STRENGTHENED AMERICA'S INTERESTS AND ALLIANCES ABROAD

+ Transformed the State Department and our approach to diplomacy to help spread democracy worldwide and combat the conditions that breed terrorism.
+ Transformed the NATO Alliance by inviting new members, launching operations around the globe, and developing 21st century capabilities.
+ Improved our relationship with China, while encouraging democratic change, transformed our alliances with democracies in East Asia, and strengthened our partnership with the European Union to advance freedom around the world.
+ Signed an historic civil nuclear agreement with India, worked with Brazil to develop and promote alternative fuels, and developed broad strategic partnerships with both countries.
+ Worked with Mexico and Central American nations to combat drug cartels and gangs and helped Colombia fight narco-terrorism and restore democratic governance.

LOWERED TAXES, INSTITUTED PRO-GROWTH POLICIES, AND ADDRESSED ECONOMIC CHALLENGES

+ Provided tax relief to every American who pays income taxes, which helped fuel more than six years of uninterrupted economic growth and 52 consecutive months of job growth.
+ Helped businesses grow and add workers by reducing the tax burden.
+ Led the response to the 2008 financial crisis.

REDUCED WASTEFUL SPENDING AND IMPROVED GOVERNMENT EFFECTIVENESS AND ACCOUNTABILITY

+ Reduced the growth of non-security discretionary spending from a rate of 16 percent to below the rate of inflation.
+ Saved taxpayers nearly $40 billion over five years through sensible entitlement reform and by terminating and reducing ineffective Federal programs.
+ Delivered transparency to the earmark process.
+ Increased the accountability, transparency, and effectiveness of the Federal Government, which improved the Government's performance and helped save billions of dollars.

IMPROVED EDUCATION FOR EVERY AMERICAN CHILD

+ Held public schools accountable, through the No Child Left Behind Act, for producing results for all students and required highly-qualified teachers in every classroom.
+ Raised reading and math scores and narrowed the achievement gap between white and minority students.
+ Provided parents with more information about school performance and choices for students stuck in low-performing schools, and created the first Federal school-choice program.
+ Increased the size of college Pell Grants to an all-time high and nearly doubled support for the Pell Grant program.
+ Established the Helping America's Youth Initiative, led by First Lady Laura Bush, to help adults connect with at-risk children.

REFORMED MEDICARE AND ADDED A PRESCRIPTION DRUG BENEFIT

+ Provided more than 40 million Americans with better access to prescription drugs through the market-based Medicare Prescription Drug Benefit.
+ Added preventive screening programs to Medicare.
+ Increased competition and choices by stabilizing and expanding Private Plan Options through the Medicare Advantage program, and increased enrollment to nearly 10 million Americans.

STRENGTHENED AMERICA'S HEALTH CARE SYSTEM

+ Empowered Americans to take charge of their health care decision-making by establishing tax-free Health Savings Accounts.
+ Infused transparency about price and quality into the health care system and launched an initiative to make electronic health records available to most Americans within 10 years.
+ Helped provide treatment to nearly 17 million people by establishing or expanding 1,200 community health centers focused in high-poverty areas.
+ Bolstered funding for medical research, which contributed to medical breakthroughs and new discoveries, including the HPV cancer vaccine.

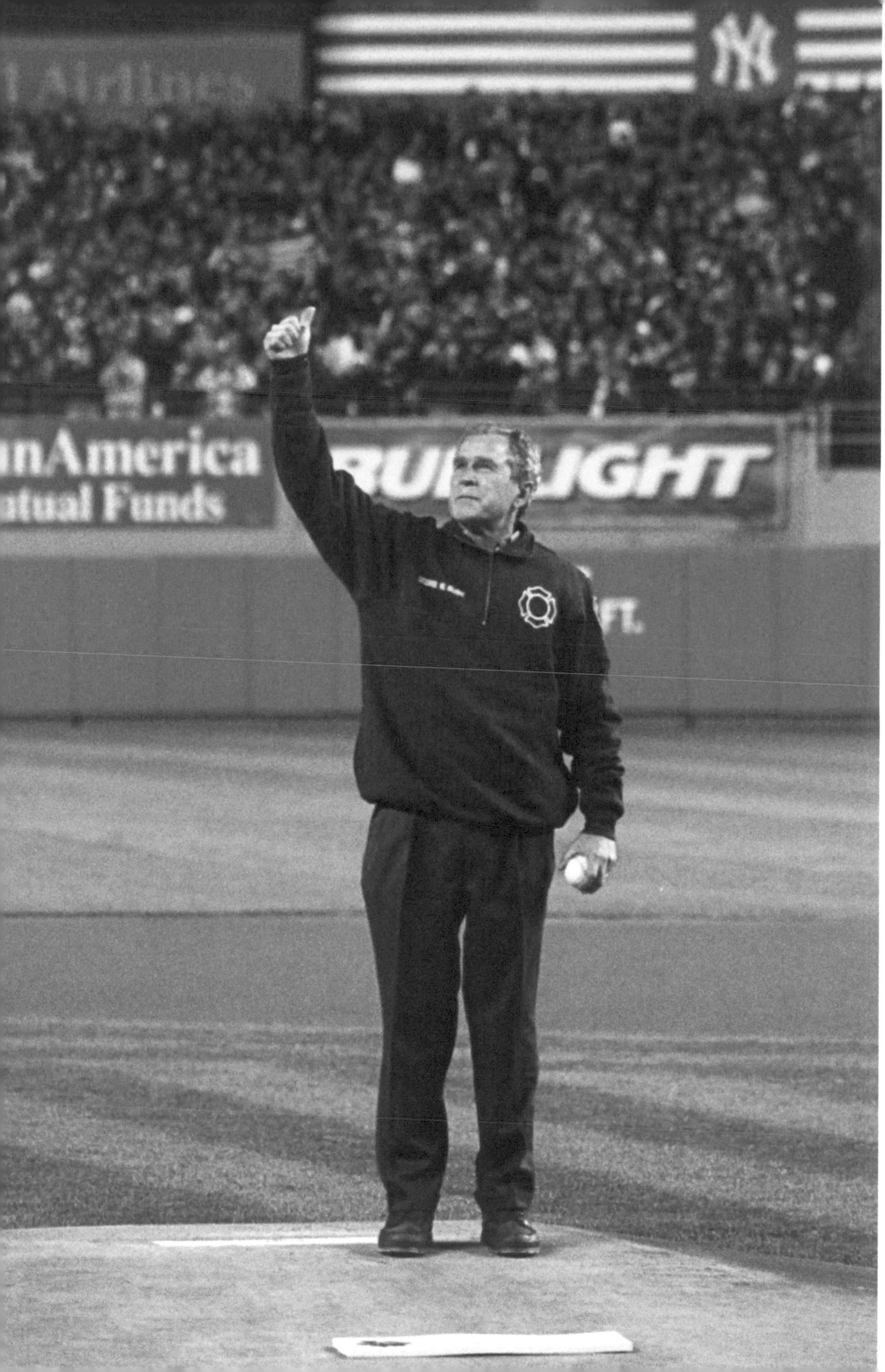

nAmerica
utual Funds
BU
IGHT

IMPROVED LIVES BY ENGAGING FAITH-BASED ORGANIZATIONS AND PROMOTING VOLUNTEERISM

+ Helped millions in need by expanding partnerships with nonprofits and leveling the playing field for faith-based and community organizations.
+ Created USA Freedom Corps following 9/11 to help Americans volunteer to serve causes greater than themselves.

PROVIDED UNPRECEDENTED RESOURCES FOR VETERANS

+ Increased total funding for the Department of Veterans Affairs more than 98 percent since 2001 and helped millions of veterans receive expedited and improved care.
+ Instituted reforms for the care of wounded warriors, many of which were based on the recommendations of the Dole-Shalala Commission, and dramatically expanded resources for mental health services.
+ Expanded education benefits for service members and veterans, increased placement and career counseling for returning veterans, and significantly reduced the processing time for disability claims.
+ Reduced the number of homeless veterans by nearly 40 percent from 2001 to 2007.

SUPPORTED AMERICAN WORKERS BY INCREASING TRADE, JOB TRAINING, AND COMPETITIVENESS

Expanded and Enforced Trade Agreements to Open New Markets for American Products

+ Leveled the playing field for American workers by increasing the number of countries partnered with the U.S. on free trade agreements from three to 14.
+ Negotiated and signed a trade agreement that helped increase U.S. exports to Central America by nearly $8 billion from 2005 to 2008.

Helped American Workers and Businesses Remain Competitive

+ Created the American Competitiveness Initiative to help Americans compete in the global economy and increased research and development funding.
+ Invested nearly $1 billion in new job training initiatives to prepare workers for 21st century jobs and ensured fair pay for American workers.

+ Helped make broadband access available in 99 percent of America's zip codes.
+ Created a new National Space Policy to ensure the continued free access and use of space for peaceful purposes and to help advance America's economic competitiveness.

SET A BRIGHT COURSE FOR AMERICA'S FUTURE

Took Unparalleled Action to Advance Cooperative Conservation and Protect the Environment

+ Created the world's largest fully protected marine area and protected our oceans by taking action to end overfishing and conserve habitats.
+ Improved and protected the health of more than 27 million acres of Federal forest and grasslands and protected, restored, and improved more than three million acres of wetlands.
+ Instituted policies that helped reduce air pollution by 12 percent from 2001 to 2007 and adopted new policies that will produce even deeper reductions.
+ Provided more than $6.5 billion to repair and improve our national parks, launched the National Parks Centennial Initiative, and established the Preserve America Initiative with First Lady Laura Bush to protect our cultural and natural heritage.

Advanced America's Energy Security and Took Steps to Develop Cleaner, More Efficient Sources of Energy

+ Called for and signed legislation to reduce U.S. gasoline consumption by tens of billions of gallons of fuel and significantly improve energy efficiency.
+ Instituted policies that helped quadruple ethanol production to more than six billion gallons.
+ Removed the executive prohibition on offshore exploration for oil and gas.
+ Provided nearly $18 billion to research, develop, and promote alternative and more efficient energy technologies such as biofuels, solar, wind, clean coal, nuclear, and hydrogen.
+ Encouraged the deployment of new nuclear reactors in the United States, which resulted in the first license applications to construct and operate new nuclear power plants in 30 years.

Reduced Crime, Lowered Teen Drug Use, Protected Vulnerable Children, and Helped Make America a More Equitable Country

+ Launched innovative strategies that contributed to the lowest overall incidence of reported crime in three decades.
+ Convicted nearly 1,300 individuals of corporate fraud and corruption.
+ Reduced drug use among teens by 25 percent.
+ Rescued more than 575 children from sexual exploitation, arrested and convicted thousands of suspects, and helped recover nearly 400 missing children since 2002 by strengthening the AMBER Alert program.
+ Protected the right to vote for generations to come by reauthorizing the Voting Rights Act and advanced civil rights.

Reduced Homelessness and Aided Struggling Homeowners

+ Reduced the number of chronically homeless people by approximately 30 percent between 2005 and 2007.
+ Helped more than two million individuals and families keep their homes by launching FHA Secure and helping to facilitate the HOPE NOW Alliance.

Improved Transportation and Import Safety and Protected American Consumers

+ Implemented congestion relief and safety measures that have made our highways and airways safer and more efficient.
+ Increased import safety for American consumers.
+ Enacted the Do Not Call List, which 145 million Americans have utilized to reduce unwanted telemarketing calls.

STOOD ON PRINCIPLE, REFUSED TO PUT OFF TOUGH DECISIONS, AND SHOWED THE WAY AHEAD

Advanced a Culture of Life

+ Outlawed partial birth abortion, ensured that every infant born alive is protected, established consequences for violence toward unborn children, and took steps to protect the rights of health care providers to act according to their conscience.
+ Provided government funding for stem cell research while refusing to sanction the destruction of human life.
+ Prohibited foreign nongovernmental organizations that receive U.S. tax dollars for family planning from performing or actively promoting abortion.

Appointed Judges Committed to Ruling by the Letter of the Law

+ Appointed Supreme Court Chief Justice John Roberts, Associate Justice Samuel Alito, and more than one-third of all active Federal judges, who will not legislate from the bench.

Confronted Climate Change through Innovation and without Harming our Economy

+ Set the country on course to stop the growth of greenhouse gas emissions below projected levels by 2025 and invested more than $44 billion in climate change-related programs.
+ Worked to build international consensus on practical actions to address climate change as a global issue.

Demonstrated Leadership on Reforming Entitlement Programs, the Immigration System, and Government Sponsored Enterprises

+ Proposed initiatives to fix Social Security and address the greatest threat to America's fiscal future—the uncontrolled growth of Federal entitlements.
+ Laid out a comprehensive plan to reform and fix our broken immigration system.
+ Warned of the risk that government-sponsored enterprises Fannie Mae and Freddie Mac posed to America's financial security beginning in 2001.

Directed Unprecedented Preparations for a Smooth Presidential Transition

+ Led the most comprehensive and forward-leaning effort in modern history to facilitate a smooth and effective transition.

Published December 2008

Printed in the USA
CPSIA information can be obtained
at www.ICGtesting.com
JSHW041934140824
68134JS00011B/122

9 781600 375828